Travel Journal

Germany

VPJournals

Copyright © 2015 VPJournals

All rights reserved.

ISBN-13: 978-1518844560
ISBN-10: 1518844561

Contact Details

Name:

Email address:

Tel:

Address:

Important Medical Information

Blood type:

Medication:

CONTENTS

Hi, I hope you enjoy this journal. It is packed with cool stuff and recommendations for you trip to Germany, and has plenty of space to record details of your trip.

What's Inside	Page
Before you go to Germany	
Great places to visit in Germany	6-7
Cool places to visit in Germany with kids	8-9
Good places to eat	10-11
Research Germany	12-13
Postcard & Packing List	14-19
Germany facts	21-22
Helpful hints	23-26
Clothes and shoe sizing charts, to help you get the right sizes while there	
Germany Trip Diary	27-111
21 day trip diary to record details of your trip	
Reflect on you Trip	
Summary of your trip	113-121
People you met	123-125
Useful Resources	127-136
Size conversion charts	129-132
Common Translations	133-134
Notes	135-136

Have fun in Germany

Great Places to visit in Germany

Neuschwanstein Castle	✓
Berg Eltz	
Kellerwald-Edersee National Park	
Pergamon Museum	
Cologne Cathedral (Kölner Dom)	
Reichstag Building	
Classic Remise Berlin	
Dresden Frauenkirche	
Gesundbrunnen Bunker	
Gemaeldegalerie	
Black Forest National Park	
Museum Island	
Ulm Münster	

Jasmund National Park	
Treptower Park	
German Historical Museum	
Hohenzollern Castle	
Berlin Hohenschoenhausen Memorial	
Palace of Tears	
Topography of Terror	
Tiergarten	
Haus der Wannsee-Konferenz	
Gemaldegalerie Alte Meister	
Zwinger	
Neues Museum Berlin	

Cool Places to visit in Germany with Kids

Europa-Park Theme Park	✓
Phantasialand Theme Park	
Hamburg Zoo	
Heide Park Theme Park	
Legoland Deutschland	
Zoologischer Garten Berlin (Zoo)	
Holiday Park (Amusement Park)	
German Museum of Technology Berlin (Deutsches Technikmuseum Berlin)	
Serengeti Park (Safari Park)	
Park Planten un Blomen Hamburg	
Bayern-Park (Amusement Park)	

Verden Magic Park (Amusement Park)	
Therme Erding (Water Park)	
Nürburgring (Motor racing)	
Designpanoptikum Berlin (Museum)	
Miniatur Wunderland (Model railways)	
Botanischer Garten Berlin	
Hansa Park (Amusement Park)	
Neues Museum Berlin	
Tropical Islands Resort	
Erlebnispark Tripsdrill (Theme Park)	
Movie Park Germany (Theme Park)	
Staatliche Kunstsammlungen Dresden (Dresden Art Galleries)	

Good Places to Eat in Germany

Heising	✓
Bar Katia & Dani	
Madami - Mom's Vietnamese Kitchen	
Bieberbau	
Jamme Ja - Italian Street Food	
Naxos Taverna	
Broeding	
Vinpasa	
Taverna Limani	
Restaurant Ilios	
Restaurant Haerlin	
Fardi Syrian Restaurant	

Restaurant Hala	
Zwickl - Gastlichkeit am Viktualienmarkt	
Lokal 1	
Restaurant Medici	
Matsuri	
Ariston	
Atschel	
Trattoria i Siciliani	
Mr Cake Cup Cakes	
Pasta Bar	
Zippiri Gourmetwerkstatt & Wein-Bar	
Amabile	
Le Moissonnier	

Best Websites to Research Further

Do some more research on the internet to plan your trip:

www.wikipedia.org/wiki/Germany
www.germany.travel
www.visitberlin.de
www.lonelyplanet.com/Germany
www.germanytravelguide.co.uk
www.justgermany.org
www.nomadicmatt.com/travel-guides/Germany-travel-tips/
www.wikitravel.org/en/Germany
www.about-germany.org

More places I want to visit on our trip

1.
2.
3.
4.
5.
6.
7.
8.
9.
10.
11.
12.
13.
14.
15.

Postcard List

Name:
Address:

Name:
Address:

Name:
Address:

Name:

Address:

Name:

Address:

Name:

Address:

Name:

Address:

Name:
Address:

Name:
Address:

Name:
Address:

Name:
Address:

Name:

Address:

Name:

Address:

Name:

Address:

MAIL

Packing List

✓	This Journal
	Tickets
	Passport
	Money
	Chargers
	Batteries
	Book to read
	Camera
	Tablet
	Sun glasses
	Sun cream

	Toiletries
	Water
	Watch
	Snacks
	Umbrella
	Towel
	Guide book
	Kindle
	Jacket
	Medication
	Add more below

Germany Facts

- Germany's official name is Bundesrepublik Deutschland (Federal Republic of Germany)

- There are over 300 different kinds of bread in Germany

- There are more football (soccer) fan clubs in Germany than anywhere else in the world

- The highest mountain in Germany is the Zugspitze at 2,963 meters (roughly 10,000 feet)

- The Black Forest is Germany's biggest nature park

- Europa Park is Germany's biggest park and the second biggest in Europe

- Germany the world's second largest producer of cars
- In the 1920s, gummy bears were invented by Hans Riegel, owner of the German candy company Haribo

- The longest word published in the German language is Donaudampfschifffahrtselektrizitätenhauptbetriebswerkbauunterbeamtengesellschaft (79 letters)

- The Christmas tree tradition came from Germany, if you are holiday there around Christmas make sure you visit some of their amazing Christmas Markets

- Zoologischer Garten Berlin (Berlin Zoological Garden) was opened in 1844 and is the oldest zoo in Germany. It holds the most comprehensive collection of species in the world

- Albert Einstein, the most recognized scientist in the world, was German and born in Ulm

- Movie Park is a film and attraction park, it actually produces movies and TV shows, you can learn all about the process if you visit

- Germans really do love beer; they rank second in world-wide beer consumption per person

- Cologne Cathedral is the third tallest cathedral in the world, it is Germany's most visited landmark, attracting an average of 20,000 people a day. It took 632 years to build

Clothes & Shoe Sizes

Children's Shoe Sizes

UK	EUROPE	US	Japan
4	20	4½ or 5	12 ½
4 ½	21	5 or 5½	13
5	21 or 22	5½ or 6	13 ½
5 ½	22	6	13½ or 14
6	23	6½ or 7	14 or 14½
6 ½	23 or 24	7 ½	14½ or 15
7	24	7½ or 8	15
7 ½	25	8 or 9	15 ½
8	25 or 26	8½ or 9	16
8 ½	26	9 ½	16 ½
9	27	9½ or 10	16 ½ or 17
10	28	10½ or 11	17 ½
10½ or 11	29	11½ or 12	18
11 ½	30	12½	18 or 18 ½
12	31	13	19 or 19 ½
12 ½	31	13 or 13½	19 ½ or 20
13	32	1	20
13 ½	32 ½	1 ½	20 ½
1	33	1½ or 2	21
2	34	2½ or 3	22

Children's Clothing Sizes

UK	EUROPE	US	Australia
12m	80cm	12-18m	12m
18m	80-86cm	18-24m	18m
24m	86-92cm	23-24m	2
2-3	92-98cm	2T	3
3-4	98-104cm	4T	4
3-5	104-110cm	5	5
5-6	110-116cm	6	6
6-7	116-122cm	6X-7	7
7-8	122-128cm	7 to 8	8
8-9	128-134cm	9 to 10	9
9-10	134-140cm	10	10
10-11	140-146cm	11	11
11-12	146-152cm	14	12

Women's Shoe Sizes

UK	EUROPE	US	Japan
3	35 ½	5	22 ½
3 ½	36	5 ½	23
4	37	6	23
4 ½	37 ½	6 ½	23 ½
5	38	7	24
5 ½	39	7 ½	24
6	39 ½	8	24 ½
6 ½	40	8 ½	25
7	41	9 ½	25 ½
7 ½	41 ½	10	26
8	42	10 ½	26 ½

Women's Clothes Sizes

UK	US	Japan	France / Spain	Germany	Germany	Australia
6/8	6	7-9	36	34	40	8
10	8	9-11	38	36	42	10
12	10	11-13	40	38	44	12
14	12	13-15	42	39	46	14
16	14	15-17	44	40	48	16
18	16	17-19	46	42	50	18
20	18	19-21	48	44	52	20

Men's Shoe Sizes

UK	EUROPE	US	Japan
6	38 ½	6 ½	24 ½
6 ½	39	7	25
7	40	7 ½	25 ½
7 ½	41	8	26
8	42	8 ½	27 ½
8 ½	43	9	27 ½
9	43 ½	9 ½	28
9 ½	44	10	28 ½
10	44	10 ½	28 ½
10 ½	44 ½	11	29
11	45	12	29 ½

Men's Suit / Coat / Sweater Sizes

UK / US / Aus	EU / Japan	General
32	42	Small
34	44	Small
36	46	Small
38	48	Medium
40	50	Large
42	52	Large
44	54	Extra Large
46	56	Extra Large

Men's Pants / Trouser Sizes (Waist)

UK / US	Europe
32	81 cm
34	86 cm
36	91 cm
38	97 cm
40	102 cm
42	107 cm

We have included another copy of this at the back of the book, so you can find it quickly again when you are in Germany

Germany Trip Diary

Write a daily diary during your trip

Day 1

Date: _____   **Weather:** _____

Day 2

Date: _____   **Weather:** _____

Day 3

Date: _____ **Weather:** _____

Day 4

Date: _____ **Weather:** _____

Day 5

Tip! Send your postcards

Date: _____   **Weather:** _____

Day 6

Date: _____   **Weather:** _____

Day 7

Date: _____   **Weather:** _____

Day 8

Date: **Weather:**

Day 9

Date: _____ **Weather:** _____

Day 10

Date: _____   **Weather:** _____

Day 11

Date: _____ **Weather:** _____

Day 12

Date: _____ **Weather:** _____

Day 13

Date: _____   **Weather:** _____

Day 14

Date: **Weather:**

Day 15

Date: _____ **Weather:** _____

Day 16

Date: **Weather:**

Day 17

Date: _____   **Weather:** _____

Day 18

Date: _____ **Weather:** _____

Day 19

Date: **Weather:**

Day 20

Date: _____   **Weather:** _____

Day 21

Date: _____   **Weather:** _____

Memories of your Trip

Things I will remember from the trip

Favorite Places visited on the Trip

People I Met

Name:
Address:
Tel:
email:

Name:
Address:
Tel:
email:

Name:
Address:
Tel:
email:

Name:
Address:
Tel:
email:

Name:
Address:
Tel:
email:

Name:
Address:
Tel:
email:

Name:
Address:
Tel:
email:

Name:
Address:
Tel:
email:

Name:
Address:
Tel:
email:

Name:
Address:
Tel:
email:

Name:
Address:
Tel:
email:

We hope you enjoyed your trip to Germany

Please leave us a review if you found this Journal useful

Check out our useful resources on the next few pages

Clothes & Shoe Sizes

Children's Shoe Sizes

UK	EUROPE	US	Japan
4	20	4½ or 5	12 ½
4 ½	21	5 or 5½	13
5	21 or 22	5½ or 6	13 ½
5 ½	22	6	13½ or 14
6	23	6½ or 7	14 or 14½
6 ½	23 or 24	7 ½	14½ or 15
7	24	7½ or 8	15
7 ½	25	8 or 9	15 ½
8	25 or 26	8½ or 9	16
8 ½	26	9½	16 ½
9	27	9½ or 10	16 ½ or 17
10	28	10½ or 11	17 ½
10½ or 11	29	11½ or 12	18
11 ½	30	12½	18 or 18 ½
12	31	13	19 or 19 ½
12 ½	31	13 or 13½	19 ½ or 20
13	32	1	20
13 ½	32 ½	1 ½	20 ½
1	33	1½ or 2	21
2	34	2½ or 3	22

Children's Clothing Sizes

UK	EUROPE	US	Australia
12m	80cm	12-18m	12m
18m	80-86cm	18-24m	18m
24m	86-92cm	23-24m	2
2-3	92-98cm	2T	3
3-4	98-104cm	4T	4
3-5	104-110cm	5	5
5-6	110-116cm	6	6
6-7	116-122cm	6X-7	7
7-8	122-128cm	7 to 8	8
8-9	128-134cm	9 to 10	9
9-10	134-140cm	10	10
10-11	140-146cm	11	11
11-12	146-152cm	14	12

Women's Shoe Sizes

UK	EUROPE	US	Japan
3	35 ½	5	22 ½
3 ½	36	5 ½	23
4	37	6	23
4 ½	37 ½	6 ½	23 ½
5	38	7	24
5 ½	39	7 ½	24
6	39 ½	8	24 ½
6 ½	40	8 ½	25
7	41	9 ½	25 ½
7 ½	41 ½	10	26
8	42	10 ½	26 ½

Women's Clothes Sizes

UK	US	Japan	France / Spain	Germany	Germany	Australia
6/8	6	7-9	36	34	40	8
10	8	9-11	38	36	42	10
12	10	11-13	40	38	44	12
14	12	13-15	42	39	46	14
16	14	15-17	44	40	48	16
18	16	17-19	46	42	50	18
20	18	19-21	48	44	52	20

Men's Shoe Sizes

UK	EUROPE	US	Japan
6	38 ½	6 ½	24 ½
6 ½	39	7	25
7	40	7 ½	25 ½
7 ½	41	8	26
8	42	8 ½	27 ½
8 ½	43	9	27 ½
9	43 ½	9 ½	28
9 ½	44	10	28 ½
10	44	10 ½	28 ½
10 ½	44 ½	11	29
11	45	12	29 ½

Men's Suit / Coat / Sweater Sizes

UK / US / Aus	EU / Japan	General
32	42	Small
34	44	Small
36	46	Small
38	48	Medium
40	50	Large
42	52	Large
44	54	Extra Large
46	56	Extra Large

Men's Pants / Trouser Sizes (Waist)

UK / US	Europe
32	81 cm
34	86 cm
36	91 cm
38	97 cm
40	102 cm
42	107 cm

Common Translations

English	French	Spanish	Italian
Hello	Bonjour	Hola	Ciao
Goodbye	Au revoir	Adiós	Arrivederci
Yes	Oui	Sí	Si
No	Non	No	No
Please	S'il-vous-plaît	Por favor	Per favore
Thank you	Merci	Gracias	Grazie
Excuse me	Excusez-moi	Perdón	Mi scusi
How much	Combien	Cuánto	Quanto
My name is	Mon nom est	Mi nombre es	Io mi chiamo
Where is	Où est	Dónde está	Dov'è
The bank	La banque	El banco	La banca
The toilet	Les toilettes	El baño	Il bagno

German	Japanese	Mandarin	Hindi
Hallo	Kon'nichiwa	Ni hao	Namaste
Auf Wiedersehen	Sayonara	Zaijian	Alavida
Ja	Hai	Shi de	Ham
Nein	Ie	Meiyou	Nahim
Bitte	Onegaishimasu	Qing	Krpaya
Vielen Dank	Arigato	Xiexie	Dhan'yavada
Entschuldigung	Sumimasen	Duoshao	Mujhe mapha karem
Wie viel	Ikura	Wo de mingzi shi	Kitana
Mein Name ist	Watashinonamaeha	Nali	Mera nama hai
Wo ist	Doko ni aru	Yinhang	Kaham hai
Die Bank	Ginko	Yinhang	Bainka
Die Toilette	Toire	Cesuo	Saucalaya

Notes:

Made in the USA
Coppell, TX
01 April 2022